# You've Got This

Printed in Australia
First Printing, 2019
ISBN: 978-0-64859299-0-7
White Light Publishing
Melton, VIC, Australia 3337

whitelightpublishing.com.au

White Light
PUBLISHING

Filled with over 100 short but powerful affirmations, messages and prompting questions, 'You've got this' will ensure you have both inspiration and empowerment at your fingertips wherever you are.

The words throughout this gorgeous little book can serve as an opportunity for regular self-reflection, or even used as an oracle to assist with any guidance you may need in your life, simply by flicking to a page when the need arises.

**You've got this.** 

I will never, ever underestimate
how powerful I truly am.

I owe no one an explanation for
my choices in life.

My emotional wellbeing is my
priority now.

It is my right to create and enforce healthy boundaries.

Is this situation really as bad as my mind is making it? Or am I catastrophizing?

I've got this.

Damn, I've got this.

It's not being selfish. It's called looking after myself.

now, it's time to do what's best
for ME.

Are these feelings really mine? Or have I absorbed them from someone else?

If I say no, it means no.

(and it's okay for me to say it)

What's really holding me back?

I am not 'everyone else', and why would I want to be anyway?

Am I going to allow this to continue? I am in control here.

now, I'm going to trust my gut, which is what I should have done all along.

Is it time to go a little deeper?

(Perhaps, that's where you'll find clarity)

The unknown is often where the magic happens.

Instead of scrambling to get
your head above water, why not
try going deeper?

I have a choice. I can continue to wonder 'what if?' or I can take a risk and see what happens.

Is this really worth my energy?

Yes, I am allowed to shine.

Not only is it healthy for me to be vulnerable, it's needed now.

I am in control of my thoughts.

It's time to stop doubting
myself.

Not everyone is going to
understand, and that's okay.

If you want this new door to open, you need to first close the ones behind you.

It's okay to be scared. That
means you're about to do
something brave.

Sometimes it hurts you more to hold on, than it does to let go.

I am more than enough.

Is it time to put your assertive
pants on now?

Who is someone in your life that just seems to 'get' you on every level? Have you thanked them?

There are some things I have no control over, and it's healthier for me to accept that.

Too late? Pfft! It's time to start following that dream now.

I don't have 'too many things to do'; I just need to prioritise them.

Some things; some people, need to just wait. I come first.

The future isn't set in stone yet; it never is. You always have a choice - and it may simply be to change your mindset.

It really is okay, to not be okay.

Will I keep wondering, 'what if?'
or will I see what happens?

Today, I'm choosing to do what
makes me happy.

(and I won't feel guilty for it)

Why are you hiding this part of yourself?

Conflict can be confronting, but sometimes it's necessary.

How someone perceives my truth
is not my concern, so long as it's
actually MY truth.

I don't always have to be the
peacekeeper.

When I reflect on all I've experienced, I draw strength from what I've learned.

I will no longer tolerate other people's bullshit.

I know that asking for help is a
sign of strength.

I can and will get through this challenge.

It's okay to let others' learn the lessons they need to for themselves, without me stepping in to 'fix' everything for them.

Say YES every now and again. You never know what you'll discover.

Change can be uncomfortable, yes. But would you rather remain where you are now?

Am I really being true to myself?

(really?)

If I take a break, the world
won't actually end.

Be mindful of your words. Are you attracting more of what you want or what you *don't* want?

What do I need to remove in order to make room for something better?

What am I carrying that isn't mine?

If I want it badly enough, I'll do something to make it happen.

Yes, I can.

Sometimes, people are only meant
to be in your life until you've each
learned what you needed to learn.

Forgiveness, when practiced only verbally, is useless. You have to mean it with all of your soul.

It is healthy for me to have a
good old cry sometimes.

No more procrastinating. Time to
take action.

You're waiting for a sign, aren't you? Stop relying on 'signs' and trust the biggest one you've got. Your *soul.*

In reality, I already have
everything I need. Now, what do
I WANT?

Have you changed? Good. You're meant to. No one wants to remain the same their entire life, anyway.

I'll embrace the simple moments today.

It's time to push myself a little further out of my comfort zone now.

It might happen, or it might not happen. How will you know if you don't make a decision?

What scares you more right now? Making a choice, or remaining stagnant?

Ask the question again, but this time, focus on the end result, rather than the journey there. Sit with that feeling for a while.

My pain can always, always be transformed into wisdom and strength. Trust that fact now.

It is safe for me to open up now,
and speak about my experiences.

It hurts, I know. But, the pain won't last forever.

Does this situation require action,
or should I just be allowing things
to flow right now?

Take a breath, and slow down.

Bring out your inner child today.

If I want clarity, I know that I need to take care of my physical health as well as my mental health.

My mirror reflects a courageous, empowered soul.

Being real is the best thing I can ever be.

Is it time to look at the bigger picture?

Remember that this situation
may be leading you towards
something incredible.

Just focus on now, for now.

Timing is everything. Maybe, it's just not the right time yet.

My frustration is showing me
that something needs to change.

What can you do today that's spontaneous?

I'll no longer hide any part of myself, just to please others.

# Where should my focus be right now?

If it's still on your mind, then it
needs to be addressed.

(Get it over with, already)

Perhaps it's time to walk away

(even if only temporarily)

Whatever I need to feel can come naturally now, and I won't push it away.

Is it better for me to just be silent right now?

Wishing for something is great.
Making it happen is even better

(and way more effective)

Is it time to forgive myself now?

(Yes, I can do it)

I have the ability to break unhealthy patterns.

I am allowed to slow down.

Even though I may not know it,
I inspire others just by being me.

I'm ready now.

What have I learned today?

Yes, I know who I am.

I don't need to have all the

answers

(who does?)

Sometimes, things simply don't go
the way we want them to.

(That's life)

Celebrate the small wins, because they're still wins after all.

What are you turning a blind eye to? Is it time to face it?

It's not about controlling what happens, but how you respond to what happens.

# My Affirmations

Use the following pages to add your own affirmations, words of inspiration, or notes to remind yourself of who you are and what's important to you.

# Also available

Visit our online shop:

www.whitelightshop.com

www.ingramcontent.com/pod-product-compliance
Lightning Source LLC
Chambersburg PA
CBHW060947050726
47592CB00003B/1142